S0-AGT-836

A Book Comes Together:

FROM IDEA TO LIBRARY

~

WRITTEN & PHOTOGRAPHED BY

RAYMOND BIAL

~

Bound to Stay Bound Books

JACKSONVILLE, ILLINOIS 2009

We would like to thank the following people who graciously assisted with this book by posing for photographs or providing help and advice: Anna Bial, Luke Bial, Marcia Burns, Barb Evans, Jeff Gallagher, Glenna Hartman, Julian Hartman, Jared Hatcher, Alice McGinty, Gabe Ramirez, Katie Shea, Maggie Shea, Patrick Shea, Sam Shea, Hannah Sweeney, Molly Sweeney, Sharon Zuiderveld, and the employees of Bound To Stay Bound Books.

Additional photo supplied by Werner Rebsamen.

Designed by Scott Piehl.
Printed by Production Press, Inc., Jacksonville, Illinois
Bound by Bound to Stay Bound Books, Jacksonville Illinois

ISBN 0-9718238-2-0 (Prebound)
ISBN 978-0-9718238-2-2 (Prebound)
L.C. Control Number 2002104047
© Bound To Stay Bound Books 2002
Revised 2009

This book is respectfully dedicated to librarians everywhere
who have devoted themselves to bringing books
into the lives of children.

TABLE OF CONTENTS

Books in People's Lives

Books are everywhere in America—in homes, schools, and libraries across the land. We now read many kinds of books, in many shapes and sizes. For thousands of years people have appreciated good books. However, only in the past century have they been able to surround themselves with a large number of books. Books are now so commonplace that everyone is familiar with them. Yet books are still precious, often magical objects.

Books help us to learn about ourselves and the world around us. Through books, we learn to care about other people. We also simply enjoy books that may be funny, sad, or even scary. This book will explain and show just how all the parts of a book come together.

Authors at Work

~

Physically, a book consists of more than paper and ink. A book expresses the thoughts and feelings of an author through words and occasionally pictures. The word **AUTHOR** comes from the Latin auctor, meaning "creator." Authors must be able to write well. Some authors need to have vivid imaginations. Others need to be experts on the subjects of their books.

Authors not only love writing, they enjoy learning about the world around them and sharing that knowledge with others through their books. Authors begin with an idea, because there must be a reason for writing and publishing a book—to learn about people in another country or simply to enjoy a ghost story. Today, many authors write on computers. Others continue to write out stories in notebooks. In any case, their completed work is called a **MANUSCRIPT.**

Publishers and Editors

~

An author submits, or sends, a manuscript to a **PUBLISHING COMPANY**. At this company, a **BOOK EDITOR** reads the manuscript and decides whether to accept the work for publication. The editor may share the manuscript with other editors and the publisher, who is in charge of the company. The employees who are responsible for marketing, or selling, the books may also be asked whether the company should publish the book or not.

If the publisher accepts the manuscript for publication, the editor will offer a contract to the author. This contract gives the publishing company the right to publish the manuscript. Once the editor has acquired the manuscript, she must carefully review every word, sentence, and paragraph. She looks for mistakes and suggests ways in which the writing may be better. The editor then returns the manuscript to the author for revisions, or changes. Other staff at the publishing company, including a **COPY EDITOR** and **PROOFREADER**, may also read the manuscript to make sure the writing is accurate and clear. The author may revise the manuscript many times before it is finished. Once the author has made these revisions, the manuscript will go on to the next stage.

Book Illustrators and Designers

~

While reviewing the manuscript, the editor also considers how the book will be illustrated. Artists known as **ILLUSTRATORS** create many different kinds of pictures, or illustrations, for the book. These may be photographs, watercolor paintings, pen and ink drawings, and many other kinds of art work. The selection of an illustrator is very important, because the pictures must help tell the story visually along with the author's words.

The editor will also choose an artist known as a **BOOK DESIGNER** who will help decide which illustrations will be best for the book. The designer will select the paper and typeface for the book. There are many kinds of typefaces which have been created over the years by artists known as **TYPOGRAPHERS.** Working with the editor, the designer will also select the most suitable cover, the dust jacket, and many other details. The designer will then lay out each of the pages of the book, carefully blending the text and the illustrations. Once the manuscript and illustrations have been completed, the book is ready to go into production.

Prepress

In the first steps of production called **PREPRESS**, all the parts of the book are prepared to be printed on a press. A **TYPESETTER** enters the text and special codes into a computer. The special codes determine exactly how each word, sentence and paragraph will appear on the finished pages of the book. In a process known as **KEYLINING**, the text and illustrations are then positioned as they will appear on each page. Much of this work is now done with computers, including **FOUR-COLOR PRINTING**. The words in a book are usually printed in black ink, but the many colors of the illustrations must also be transferred onto each page. Remarkably, all these colors are obtained from various combinations of the four primary printing colors (red, yellow, blue, and black). A technician uses a machine called a **LASER SCANNER** to make a negative, or separation, for each of the four colors. Composed of many tiny dots, each negative is a reverse picture of the illustration.

Printing the Book

The next step is **STRIPPING** in which the negatives are taped onto large plastic sheets referred to as **FLATS.** The flats are then exposed on very thin sheets of specially coated metal to make printing plates.

The printer installs these plates in a four-color printing press. He loads paper into one end of the press, pours red, yellow, blue, and black ink into four separate troughs, and then makes careful settings. As the press runs, ink flows onto the plates and then onto the paper running through the press. All the pages for thousands of copies of a book will be printed in just a few hours. The ink is allowed to dry and then the sheets are sent to the **BINDERY**.

Binding the Book

~

At the bindery the sheets of paper are gradually turned into books. The sheets are first run through a **FOLDING** machine in which they are folded again and again to make little booklets, or signatures, of sixteen or more pages. All the **SIGNATURES** that make up a book then go into a gathering machine, along with thick pages called endpapers, which are attached to the front and back of the signatures. The gathered signatures are then quickly sewn together along the folded edge, or **SPINE**, with a special machine. The edges of the sewn signatures are trimmed on a paper cutter with a large, very sharp blade.

The books will then be bound in a **CASE**, or cover, which protects the pages. Hardcover books have covers of stiff cardboard sheathed with paper or cloth. The signatures are then positioned in the cases and pressed together for a good fit. Paperback books have covers of heavy paper. Paperback books are less costly, but also less durable than hardcover books. Glue is applied to the cases as they pass through a complex machine.

The finished books are stacked, then sent to the warehouse for storage and later shipment to schools, libraries, and stores.

A Better Binding

Finished books are sold to stores where they are purchased for libraries at home. Many books, however, are acquired by schools and libraries where they are eagerly read again and again. Unfortunately, whether paperback or regular hardcover, the binding of most of these books is not strong enough to withstand such eager, repeated use.

A method of binding resulting in a more durable book, known as prebinding, has been found to serve best for library books. **PREBINDING** provides longer lasting covers for books and keeps the pages from coming apart. The very best prebound books must follow the **ANSI/NISO/LBI LIBRARY BINDING STANDARD**.

Books Arrive at Bound To Stay Bound Books

~

Bound To Stay Bound specializes in this superior method of prebinding described by the LBI. Every day thousands of books arrive at Bound To Stay Bound Books in Jacksonville, Illinois, from publishers across the United States and around the world. Many of these books have already been bound while others are received in **FOLIOS**. Folios are folded and gathered sheets, or pages, that are ready to be bound. Each of these new books must be checked in and examined to make sure that all the pages are in order and that the volume is not damaged.

A copy of each book is then moved to a desk for careful analysis. The book is measured to determine the precise margins, or white space around the text and pictures on the pages. Careful measuring also determines the size of the cover boards and the overlap of the cover fabric, as well as the amount of space needed for the hinge of the cover. The type of sewing is determined by the thickness of the book.

An instruction sheet is placed in each book which then continues its journey through the bindery.

Removing Original Book Covers

16

~

The bindery prefers to receive books in folios, or folded and gathered sheets. For these books, it is necessary only to make sure all the pages are in the proper order. However, many books arrive at Bound To Stay Bound Books already bound. The covers of these books have to be removed, either by hand or machine—depending on how the book was bound and the width of the inner margin. A worker either carefully slices the pages away from the cover or uses a guillotine cutter.

Once the covers have been removed, a worker sands the backs to remove the dried glue and lining materials. To preserve as much of the inner margin as possible, he works carefully to make a smooth edge on each book. Occasionally, if the book has a wide inner margin, it is run through a **GRINDING MACHINE** that quickly removes the back fold of each book. Finally, to keep the pages together, a light coat of glue is applied to the spine of each book.

Making New Endpapers

ENDPAPERS protect the pages and sewing of a book. At Bound To Stay Bound Books, new endpapers are applied to each book. These endpapers have four parts: a pasted-down end leaf that becomes the inside lining of the cover, two free fly leaves, and reinforcing fabric to hold all the parts together. All these parts are assembled at one time by a complex machine. Rolls of paper are fed through the machine, then automatically folded and glued to the strips of fabric.

BTSB EXTRA: Trade editions often have endpapers with just two sheets of paper and a much flimsier reinforcing fabric than is used in a Bound To Stay Bound book.

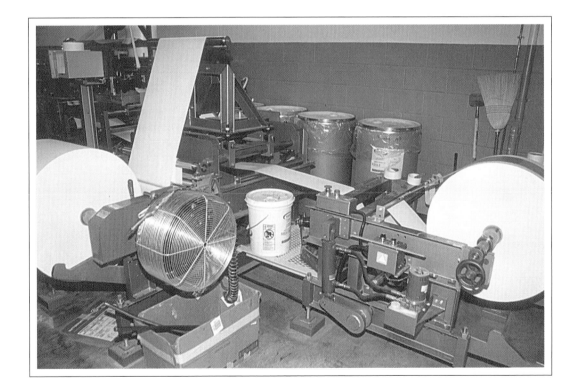

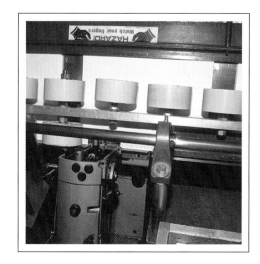  

18

Sewing the Pages Together

~

Slender books, less than a half-inch thick, are sewn together on a **SIDE SEWING MACHINE**. Just as clothing is sewn, these machines use thread to hold the pages and endpapers together in a process called **SIDE-STITCHING**. The machines tightly stitch the pages, endpapers, and reinforcing fabric together along the full length of the spine.

Thicker books, more than a half-inch thick, are **OVERSEWN**. These books have numerous sections, or booklets. Starting with the bottom endpaper, each of these parts is sewn one at a time. The book is completed when the top endpaper is sewn onto the stack of sections. Sewing each part to the adjoining parts makes for a very strong book which will never come apart.

BTSB EXTRA:
Thin trade editions are often sewn with a lightweight thread just once down the middle of the signatures, rather than tougher side sewing. Thicker trade editions are often glued, or the signatures are held together with a single thread instead of the repeated, heavy sewing used in oversewing.

19

Creasing and Sealing Endpapers

~

In the Creasing and Sealing Department, the endpapers are folded back to form a hinge for the cover. An automatic machine creases the endpapers to make them even with the back edge of the book. The fabric in the endpapers has already been treated with a heat-sealing adhesive, and this machine also seals the endpapers down using heat and pressure.

Trimming Books

~

Sewn books are now ready for final trimming along three edges—top, bottom and front. The back spine is not trimmed. In the past, all three sides of the book had to be trimmed one at a time. However, with the **THREE KNIFE TRIMMING MACHINE**, three very sharp knives are adjusted to precisely slice all three sides at once. As with virtually all the bindery equipment, this machine is electronically operated with special safety features to protect the operator from injury. The paper trimmings, along with extra materials from many other bindery operations, are sent off to a company that will recycle them into other products.

Rounding and Backing Books

~

The books are now ready for a machine called the **ROUNDER AND BACKER**. In this process, each book is fed into the hydraulically powered machine, and a heavy weight rolls across it. This machine quickly and powerfully shapes the book by squeezing the pages together and forming a slight curve on the spine.

All well bound thick books have a rounded spine, which not only strengthens the binding, but allows the pages to turn more freely.

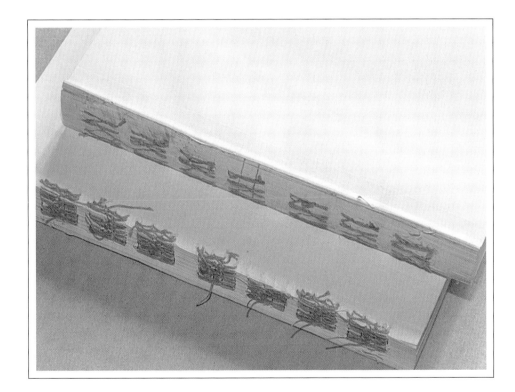

Backlining Books

~

According to standards of the Library Binding Institute, a book must have a strong backlining material before it is encased in its cover. This material consists of strong, flexible cotton cloth that wraps around the spine and extends about an inch on each side of the book. As the book moves along a conveyor belt, the backlining machine spreads glue on the spine, cuts the lining material into strips, and applies the strips to the book.

BTSB EXTRA:

Trade editions will often have a very lightweight cloth or even a paper backlining instead of the very strong cloth used by Bound To Stay Bound.

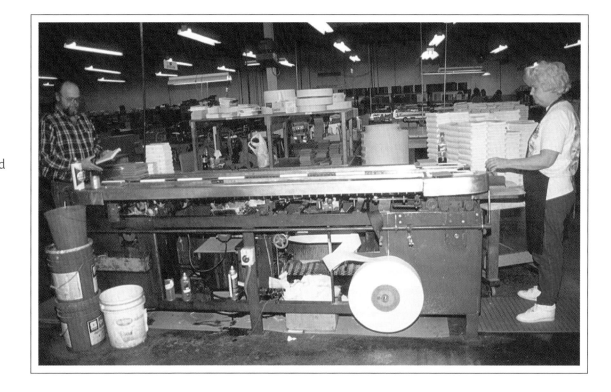

Printing
Picture Covers ™
~

A case now has to be created to wrap around the sewn pages to protect them from being damaged. The first step is to reproduce the illustration from the front of the original book onto a piece of library buckram or our specially designed Kid Proof ™ material to make a cover.

The illustration for the cover is first scanned into a computer and negatives are produced digitally. The negatives for each of the four colors are then stripped on a light table, and the negatives are used to make metal plates for the printing presses.

The cover material comes to Bound To Stay Bound Books in large rolls that need to be cut down to the proper size for every book.

Bound To Stay Bound Books uses several offset presses to transfer the image from the plate onto the cover in bright durable colors. Each time the cover passes through the printing press one color is applied to the cover. As many as four colors are printed on a single book cover.

After the ink has dried on the illustration, a protective ultraviolet (UV) coating is applied to the printed cover. This coating will protect the cover from scrapes, scratches, repeated cleaning, and other wear.

BTSB EXTRAS:

• Trade editions often have an attractive cover illustration and book description on the dust jacket only. The book's cover is left plain. Bound To Stay Bound books feature the original book illustration and description on the cover itself, so it will be visible long after the dust jacket has been torn or lost.

• The cover of a trade edition is often made from a very lightweight cloth material or a paper that has been laminated with plastic. A Bound To Stay Bound book cover is always made from a very heavyweight polyester/cotton library buckram cloth or our specially designed KidProof ™ cover material.

24

Making Book Cases

Once the cover is made, the case can be put together. A case has three other parts—two pieces of binders board and the spine inlay. Once these three items have been cut to the proper size, the cases are made by machines specially designed for this purpose or by hand in six separate steps, each by a different person, along a small assembly line.

After the glue has been applied to the binders boards and inlay strip, they are centered on the back of the covers with the help of mirrors. The four corners are turned two at a time on a special corner turning device, and then the four edges are folded over. Finally, at the far end of the table, the case goes through a roller that smoothly seals the glued areas.

Casing in the Book

~

In the process known as casing in, the finished case is joined with the book. **CASING IN** is done with a special machine on which the books are divided in the center and placed by hand. Each book is then carried between two paste wells as the cover moves above the wells. When the book comes up, it is then perfectly aligned for sliding into the cover.

After casing in, the book continues along a conveyor belt through a **BUILDING-IN MACHINE**. Under intense heat and pressure, the glue is dried and a deep groove is pressed into the book. This groove enables the book to open and close properly.

To insure that the parts fit tightly together, the book is squeezed in a large hydraulic press.

Inspecting Finished Books

After each book has been bound, it is carefully inspected. It must be properly sewn. The endpapers must be square. The library corners have to be neat and perfectly glued. There should be no rough edges and the groove must be deep enough. The covers must also be centered. A person confirms that all these and more standards are met before a book passes inspection.

She places a gold Bound To Stay Bound seal on the inside front cover as a guarantee that the book has met or exceeded all requirements for quality.

The original paper dust jacket is put back on the book and the computer inventory is updated. The book then goes to the storeroom.

Librarians Select Books

Librarians order many books for their libraries. But how do they decide whether or not to purchase a book? Librarians do not have time to read all of the thousands of books published every year. So, they read short articles called **BOOK REVIEWS**, published in various newspapers and magazines, especially professional library journals. Each of these articles is written by a **REVIEWER**, a knowledgeable person who has read the book. The reviewer briefly describes the book and then recommends whether it should be purchased or not. Reviews help librarians and teachers decide whether a book is good and appropriate for their libraries and schools. Librarians also have to be very aware of what subjects are being taught in their school's classrooms so they can have books in the library to support those subjects. Children also help choose books by making suggestions to their parents, teachers, and librarians—and then reading those books.

Librarians Place Orders

Once they have chosen the books to be added to their collections, librarians must decide from which company to order these books. Some librarians purchase books directly from the publishers, which can be very difficult considering the hundreds of publishers of children's books. Most librarians order books through wholesalers. Many librarians select Bound To Stay Bound as their **WHOLESALER** to acquire durable, cost-effective books that rarely, if ever, need to be replaced.

Since Bound To Stay Bound Books are guaranteed to circulate at least one hundred times, they far outlive other editions of the same books. For example, **TRADE EDITIONS** have been estimated by the Library Binding Institute to circulate only ten times before needing repair or replacement. **LIBRARY AND REINFORCED EDITIONS** average 25 to 30 circulations, although this may vary quite a bit because there is no industry standard to govern how they are bound. The librarian must carefully consider what edition of the book to purchase in order to make the best use of the taxpayers' investment in the library.

Orders Arrive at
Bound To Stay Bound Books

~

Orders arrive at Bound To Stay Bound Books every day. Many orders come electronically from the company website, www.btsb.com. Others arrive by fax or mail. Once an order has been received at the Order Entry Department, an employee enters the information into a computer, including the preferences of the customer. This information, including date of the order, name and address of the library, and book cataloging and processing requests, assures the librarian that she will correctly receive all the books she ordered for her library. In fact, the librarian will receive at least 85 to 90% of her order within 60 days.

Picking Books on Orders

~

With row after row of over one and a half million finished books, the vast stockroom at Bound To Stay Bound Books holds over 18,000 popular titles for children—all of which are ready for shipment. The employees responsible for filling customer orders wear roller skates. Their roller skates enable them to zip up and down the aisles, invoice in hand, quickly and accurately picking the books for each order.

Processing Books on Orders

~

Once the books have been picked from the shelves in the storeroom, they are rechecked against the invoices. This step insures that each library will receive the correct books on its order. Many books are then processed with customized catalog card sets, circulation system bar code, and security tape, along with cataloging information provided on computer disk or downloadable from our website. When requested, employees at Bound To Stay Bound Books will also laminate the original dust jackets and put them back on the books. Other employees stamp **DEWEY**, easy, and fiction classifications on book spines with hot brass type so that library patrons will be able to find the book on the shelf. Other librarians prefer to have the company apply labels with these classifications on the spine.

BTSB EXTRAS:

• Laminated Dust Jackets: The paper jackets provided with most trade editions offer added attractiveness. However, BTSB can seal those jackets between polyester film and a paper backing, fold them onto the books and tape them in place, thereby adding significant longevity to the jackets as well as the book.

• Stamped Spine: Unlike trade editions, BTSB books can be permanently imprinted with call numbers on the spines with hot brass type. This unique service is made possible due to the buckram cover material used on every BTSB book.

Packing and Shipping Books

~

Books are inspected once more, then carefully wrapped in plastic, and packed in sturdy cardboard boxes. The books are now ready to be shipped free of charge to school and library customers anywhere in the continental United States. Brown UPS trucks back up at the loading dock and carry away boxes and boxes of books to distant schools and libraries. Bound To Stay Bound Books may find a place on the shelves in libraries hundreds or even thousands of miles away.

Librarians Receive Books

~

Librarians promptly receive their orders from Bound To Stay Bound Books—usually three to five days after they leave the company. In most cases, the books are ready to be placed in the school or library upon their arrival, and children will enjoy countless hours of reading. If teachers or librarians have any questions about their orders, they can always call the efficient, helpful Customer Support Department at Bound To Stay Bound Books. Or they can get in touch with the experienced professional sales staff. The staff are always eager to acquaint people with the books and services of Bound To Stay Bound Books.

Children Love Books

~

Discovering a wonderful book on the library shelves can be a magical experience for a young person. Every day, thousands of children discover anew the pleasures of reading. They may wander through a haunted house, travel to a faraway land, or learn about dinosaurs through the pages of a good book. Each day may bring a new adventure and a fresh insight.

Book Care Tips

～

Environment

- Avoid temperature extremes. Books should ideally be kept in rooms where the temperature is not higher than 70 degrees F and no more than 50% relative humidity.

- Do not keep your books in attics, basements, garages, and areas around water pipes. Damp environments can lead to mold and mildew.

- Avoid storing your books near a heater, or in direct sunlight, because books may be damaged by extreme temperatures and harsh lighting. Heat warps books. Sunlight fades and yellows pages.

- Keep your books on metal or sealed wooden shelves. The acid in wood can damage the fibers of the paper. If possible, store your books in a glass-enclosed bookcase, for maximum protection.

- Use shelves big enough so that your books will stand up and not scrape the shelf above.

- Shelve your books upright. Leaning stresses the pages and binding. Large books can be stored horizontally or on the spine (not on the front edge).

- Be careful not to shelve your books too tightly. Crowding can break spines, and books may be damaged when retrieved.

- Place books toward the front edge of bookshelves, which allows air to circulate behind them.

- Place a few whole cloves in the corners of bookshelves to prevent mildew.

- Dust your books at least once a year. Remove each volume from the shelf and, while the book is tightly closed, brush with a wide soft-bristled paint brush.

Handling With Care

- Take your books from the shelves carefully. Do not pull on the top edge of the spine which may be damaged. Instead push in the books on either side and then pull from the middle of the book you want to read.

- Read your books with clean hands.

- Keep food and drinks away from your books. They can stain books, as well as attract insects and rodents.

- Don't lay open books face down to keep your place. Use a bookmark and close the book.

- Use a flat bookmark to keep your place, not metal paper clips or other bulky objects, and never turn down the corners.

- Never write in or otherwise mark a book, especially one that does not belong to you.

- Do not use a book as a surface upon which to write. The impression made under your paper damages the book.

- When photocopying a book do not push the spine down. It may crack the spine.

- MOST IMPORTANTLY, enjoy reading your books each and every day.

Anatomy of a Book

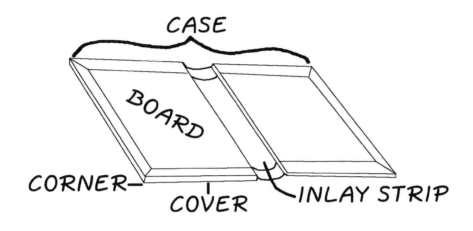

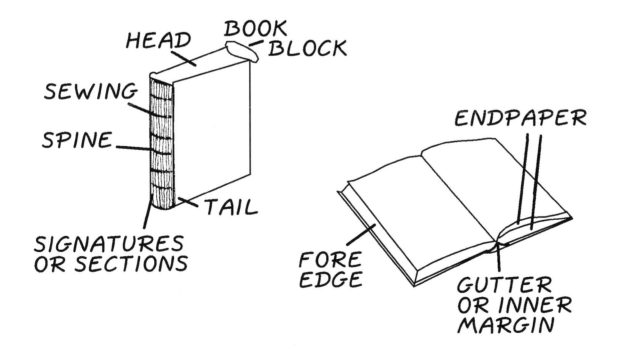

Glossary

~

ANSI/NISO/LBI Standard for Library Binding:
American National Standards Institute/National
Information Standards Organization/Library Binding
Institute Z39.78-2000 describes the technical specifications
and materials specifications for Library Binding.

AUTHOR: person who writes a book, from the Latin
auctor, meaning creator.

BINDERY: company where books are bound in paperback
or hardcover.

BOOK DESIGNER: person who selects the paper and
typeface, determines the layout, and helps choose the
illustrations for a book.

BOOK EDITOR : individual who accepts an author's work
for publication and suggests revisions of the manuscript.

BOOK REVIEW: article published in a newspaper or magazine
that evaluates the quality of a book.

BUILDING-IN-MACHINE: a machine that takes a book after
it has been cased in and , using high heat and pressure,
makes sure the book is securely connected to the case.

CASE: the cover which protects the pages of a book.

CASING IN: The process of joining the sewn or glued
pages of a book with its outer cover or case.

COPY EDITOR: person who makes sure the writing
is accurate and clear in a manuscript prior to publication.

DEWEY DECIMAL SYSTEM: method of classifying books
by subject within a library collection.

ENDPAPERS: thick sheets of paper that are glued to the
inside cover of a book to attach the cover to the pages.

FLATS: large plastic sheets on which the film of each page
of a book is taped.

FOLDING: process through which printed sheets are folded
into booklets, or signatures, of sixteen or more pages.

FOLIO: folded and gathered sheets, or pages, of a book
that are ready to be bound.

FOUR-COLOR PRINTING: sophisticated process of printing
photographs and other color illustrations from various
combinations of the four primary printing colors (red,
yellow, blue, and black).

GRINDING MACHINE: a machine with a rotating knife used
to take off part of the spine of the book.

ILLUSTRATOR: artist who creates watercolors, drawings,
photographs, or other kinds of pictures called illustrations.

KEYLINING: process, now done by computer, in which the
text and illustrations are positioned as they will appear
on each page of a book.

LASER SCANNER: a machine that analyzes every detail of
an illustration with intense beams of light. A scan is made
for each of the four colors, then four negatives. Composed
of many tiny dots, each negative is a reverse picture of the
illustration.

LIBRARY BINDING INSTITUTE: organization that sets the high standard for prebound books.

LIBRARY EDITION: book bound with heavier materials than a trade edition, which may average 25 to 30 circulations, although this estimate may vary quite a bit because there is no industry standard. Also known as reinforced edition.

MANUSCRIPT: written or typewritten composition, an author's completed, unpublished work.

OVERSEWING: method of sewing the signatures of thick books, more than a half-inch thick, one on top of the other for greater strength.

PREBINDING: form of durable binding that protects the covers of books and keeps the pages from coming apart, produced according to the standard of the Library Binding Institute.

PREPRESS: all the steps in preparing the parts of a book to be printed on a press.

PROOFREADER: individual who corrects misspellings and other errors in a manuscript.

PUBLISHING COMPANY: company which publishes books and other materials.

REVIEWER: individual who writes an evaluation of a book that is published in a newspaper or magazine.

ROUNDER AND BACKER: a machine in which a heavy weight rolls across the spine of a book to give it a slightly curved shape.

SIDE-STITCHING: method of sewing the pages, endpapers, and reinforcing fabric together along the full length of the spine, also known as side sewing.

SIGNATURE: printed sheet that has been folded into a small booklet.

SPINE: the back edge of a book.

STRIPPING: taping of negatives in the correct position onto large plastic sheets called flats.

THREE KNIFE TRIMMING MACHINE: a machine that can trim the three sides of a book, not including the spine, all at the same time.

TRADE EDITION: book commonly bound with lightweight materials which may be expected to circulate only ten times before needing repair or replacement.

TYPESETTER: person who keys, or transfers, the text into a computer along with codes, or commands, that determine the typeface, size of the type, and other elements of the design.

TYPOGRAPHER: artist who creates new styles of typefaces.

WHOLESALER: company that buys large quantities of books from many publishers and then resells them to libraries and bookstores.

Further Reading

Brookfield, Karen. *Book*. New York: Dorling Kindersley, 2000.

Marshall, Pam A. *From Idea to Book*. Minneapolis: Lerner, 2004.

Petterchak, Janice A. *"Books that Stand the Test of Time:" The Story of Bound To Stay Bound Books, 1920-1998*. Jacksonville, IL: Bound To Stay Bound Books, 1998.

Summerfield, Melvin B. *The Book That Had a Secret*. Jacksonville, IL: Bound To Stay Bound Books, 1965.

About the Author

Raymond Bial (pronounced *Beal*) is the author and photo-illustrator of more than a hundred critically-acclaimed books for children and adults, including *Amish Home, Frontier Home, The Underground Railroad, Where Lincoln Walked, Where Washington Walked, A Handful of Dirt, Ghost Towns of the American West, Tenement: Immigrant Life on the Lower East Side, Nauvoo: Mormon City on the Mississippi River, The Super Soybean, Ellis Island: Coming to the Land of Liberty,* and many others. His subjects range from farm life to American social and cultural history. He has also written three popular collections of mystery fiction for children: *The Fresh Grave and Other Ghostly Stories* and *The Ghost of Honeymoon Creek* and most recently *Shadow Island: A Tale of Lake Superior,* published by Bluehorse Books. His books have received numerous awards from the American Library Association, National Council of Teachers of English, Children's Book Council, and many other organizations. He lives with his wife, Linda, and children, Sarah and Luke, in Urbana, Illinois. His daughter Anna, who illustrated two of Raymond's books, is a fashion designer in New York City.